*Your word is a lamp for my feet,
and a light for my path.*
Psalm 119:105

To:

_____

From:

_____

Date:

_____

MY FIRST BIBLE

CATHOLIC EDITION

Edited by
Bart Tesoriero

Nihil Obstat
Right Reverend Archimandrite Francis Vivona,
S.T.M., J.C.L.

Imprimatur
Most Reverend Joseph A. Pepe, D.D., J.C.D.

Date
March 18, 2014
Saint Cyril of Jerusalem

ISBN 1-61796-120-5
© 2014 Aquinas Kids, Phoenix, Arizona
Printed in China

Table of Contents

God Creates the Heavens and the Earth................4

Adam and Eve 6

The Fall of Adam and Eve 8

Noah and the Ark......................................10

God calls Abram 12

Jacob and Esau...14

Joseph and the Coat of Many Colors..................16

Joseph Saves His People 18

The Birth of Moses 20

God Sets His People Free 22

The Ten Commandments 24

Israel Enters the Promised Land 26

Samuel Hears the Voice of God 28

David and Goliath.....................................30

The Temple of Solomon..............................32

Jonah and the Whale..................................34

Daniel and the Lions' Den 36

The Annunciation 38

The Journey to Bethlehem 40

The Birth of Jesus 42

The Gift of the Magi..................................44

The Finding of Jesus in the Temple 46

The Baptism of Jesus 48

Jesus Calls His Apostles 50
The Wedding at Cana..52
The Sermon on the Mount 54
Jesus Cures a Leper..56
Jesus Teaches His Disciples to Pray 58
Jesus Calms the Storm...60
The Miracle of the Loaves and Fishes 62
Jesus Names Peter as the Rock..................................64
Jesus Heals a Little Girl 66
Jesus Blesses the Children 68
The Good Samaritan 70
The Forgiving Father 72
Blind Bartimaeus 74
The Good Shepherd..76
Jesus Enters Jerusalem 78
Jesus Cleanses the Temple 80
The Last Supper..82
The Agony in the Garden..84
Jesus is Condemned to Death 86
Jesus Dies on the Cross 88
Jesus Rises from the Dead! 90
Jesus Ascends into Heaven 92
The Holy Spirit Descends Upon the Apostles 94
The Gospel Spreads to the Whole World............96

THE OLD TESTAMENT
God Creates the Heavens and the Earth

In the beginning, a long, long time ago, before
the world was made, even before there was the
sky, or the sun, or the moon, there was God.

God is like a family: the Father, the Son, and
the Holy Spirit. He was completely happy, yet
He wanted to share His happiness with others.
God wanted a family, with whom He could
share His love. He decided to create people!

First of all, God made a place where men,
women, and children could live. God created
the heavens and the earth. He made the sun
and the moon, the stars and the seas, the trees
and the plants, the birds and the fishes, and
all the animals and creatures of the earth. God
looked at all He had made, and He said, "It is
good!"

Adam and Eve

Then God created the parents of us all, Adam and Eve. He made them in His image and likeness. God placed Adam and Eve in a beautiful paradise called the Garden of Eden. He told them to take care of the Garden. Sweet-smelling flowers and ripe, juicy fruits grew everywhere. Lively birds sang in the trees and the animals all romped and played together.

God told Adam and Eve that they could eat the fruit of every tree in the Garden except for the tree of the knowledge of good and evil. He told them that if they ate from it, they would die.

When God finished creating Adam and Eve, He said, "Now that is very good!" God made everything in six days. On the seventh day, God rested from His work, and He blessed the day. That day is called the Sabbath.

The Fall of Adam and Eve

One day the devil came in the form of a snake to tempt Eve. He told her that if she ate the forbidden fruit, she would become like God. Eve saw that the fruit looked tasty, so she decided to eat it. She then gave it to Adam, who also ate it. When they ate it, they realized they had displeased God by disobeying Him.

Almighty God was very unhappy with Adam and Eve. They had lost His presence in their hearts, and they could no longer stay in the beautiful Garden. God told the snake that he would have to crawl around on his belly and stay away from all the other animals and wild creatures. But God also promised to send a Redeemer to save all people, a Savior who would be born of a woman. The Redeemer would crush the head of the snake, and the snake would strike at his heel.

Noah and the Ark

Adam and Eve had many children, who spread out over the face of the earth. People forgot about God. They sinned and became wicked. God became angry and told a good man named Noah that He had decided to put an end to everyone living on the earth, because they were wicked. He told Noah to build a large boat called an ark, because He was going to send a flood upon the earth. God told Noah to go into the ark with his wife, his sons and their wives, and two of each kind of animal, one male and one female.

God sent a flood upon the earth. It rained for forty days and forty nights, and only Noah and all who were in the ark were saved. After the flood was over, Noah offered a sacrifice to thank God for His goodness. God put a rainbow in the sky as a sign that He would never again destroy the earth with a flood.

God Calls Abram

Many years after Noah, God called a holy man named Abram to leave his country and his father's family, and to go into a land that He would show him. God promised to make of Abram and his wife Sarai a great nation, and to bless them with great blessings.

God promised Abram that his wife would give birth to a son, and they named the boy Isaac. God changed Abram's name to Abraham, which means "the father of many nations."

One day, God told Abraham to offer his son, Isaac, as a sacrifice to Him. Abraham obeyed, but God sent an angel to stop him. God told Abraham, "Because you did not hold back from Me your beloved son, I will bless you abundantly and give you more descendants than the stars of heaven!"

Jacob and Esau

Abraham died as a friend of God. Isaac married Rebecca and she gave birth to twins, Esau, her firstborn, and Jacob. Esau grew to be a hunter, who lived out in the open. Jacob was a simple man, who preferred living in tents.

One day Esau traded his birthright as firstborn son to Jacob in return for a bowl of stew. Rebecca tricked Isaac into thinking that Jacob was Esau, and with a special blessing, Isaac made Jacob his heir. Esau was very angry, so Jacob left home.

That night, Jacob dreamed of a ladder from earth to heaven, with the angels of God going up and down its steps. The Lord stood beside Jacob and promised to fulfill all His promises to Abraham and Isaac. Jacob set up a memorial stone at that place and called it Bethel, which means, "the house of God."

Joseph and the Coat of Many Colors

Jacob had twelve sons, including Joseph, who was born when Jacob was old. Jacob loved Joseph very much, and made him a coat of many colors. Joseph's brothers became jealous and angry with him. One day Jacob sent Joseph out to the fields to visit his brothers. They tied him up and sold him to some traders as a slave. They dipped his coat in the blood of a goat and sent it to Jacob, who thought that a wild beast had killed and eaten his son.

The traders sold Joseph to a man who served the Pharaoh, or ruler, of Egypt. One day the man's wife tried to get Joseph to sin. He refused and she had him thrown into jail. After a long time, Joseph was released and ended up serving the Pharaoh as the governor of Egypt.

Joseph Saves His People

God told Joseph through a dream of the Pharaoh that there would be seven years of plenty and seven years of famine in the land. Therefore Joseph had the people store up grain so they would have food to eat.

Jacob sent his sons to Egypt to buy grain. Joseph recognized his brothers, but they did not recognize him. Joseph told them, "I am Joseph, your brother! How is my father Jacob?" Joseph wept loudly and embraced his brothers, gave them wonderful gifts, and sent them home to their father. When Jacob learned that his beloved son was still alive, he came to see him. Joseph ran to embrace him, weeping. "Now I can die with joy," said Jacob, "because I have seen your face." Joseph gave land to his father and brothers, and they became a great nation in Egypt.

The Birth of Moses

Many years passed. A new Pharaoh ruled
Egypt, and he was afraid that the Hebrews
would become more powerful than his own
people. He made them his slaves. He also
commanded that every Hebrew baby boy be
drowned in the Nile River.

A certain Hebrew woman gave birth to a little
boy, whom she loved very much. She made a
basket out of plant leaves and sorrowfully put
the basket among the reeds near the river. Her
daughter Miriam hid in the bushes to watch.

The Pharaoh's daughter came down to the
river to bathe, and was greatly surprised find
a little baby boy floating in a basket. She
decided to keep him and raise him as her own
son. She called his name Moses, which means
'saved out of the water.'

God Sets His People Free

Moses grew up in the house and court of the Pharaoh. One day, he killed an Egyptian man for hitting a Hebrew man, and then he fled to Arabia. God appeared in a burning bush to Moses. He told him, "I am the God of Abraham, Isaac, and Jacob. I will send you to Pharaoh to lead My people, Israel, out of Egypt to the Promised Land."

Moses and his brother Aaron told the Pharaoh, "Thus says the LORD: 'Let My people go, so they can worship Me.'" But Pharaoh refused, so God sent ten plagues upon Egypt. Finally the Pharaoh let the Israelites go, but then he chased them to the Red Sea. Moses told the people, "Be not afraid! The LORD himself will fight for you!" He stretched out his staff, and God parted the Sea. The Hebrews passed over on dry ground, but the water flowed back and covered the Egyptians. Not a single one escaped.

The Ten Commandments

Three months after leaving Egypt, the Israelites came to Mount Sinai. God called Moses up to the mountain and told him to tell the people that if they remained faithful to the Lord, He would continue to protect them and would make them His own chosen people.

Then God delivered to Moses the Ten Commandments:
"I am the Lord your God. You shall not have other gods besides Me. You shall not take the name of the LORD, your God, in vain. Remember to keep holy the Sabbath day. Honor your father and your mother. You shall not kill. You shall not commit adultery. You shall not steal. You shall not bear false witness against your neighbor. You shall not desire your neighbor's wife. You shall not desire your neighbor's goods."

Israel Enters the Promised Land

After Moses died, the Lord commanded Joshua to lead the Israelites into Canaan. They needed to capture Jericho, a large city with strong walls. God commanded the people to march around Jericho for seven days, led by the priests who were to carry the Ark of the Covenant—a great wooden box covered with gold, which contained the tablets of the Law.

For six days the priests sounded the trumpets, but the people remained silent. On the seventh day, Joshua told the people to march around the city seven times, and the seventh time to shout as the priests blew their horns. At the sound of the trumpets and the shouts of the people, the walls of Jericho came tumbling down and the Israelites captured the city! In time, Israel took possession of the land which God had promised to Abraham forever.

Samuel Hears the Voice of God

When the Israelites settled in the Promised Land, they forgot their promise to God, and began to worship other gods. When this happened, God allowed their enemies to defeat them. Then the Hebrews cried out to God, and He sent holy men and women, called Judges, to deliver them and rule them.

The last of these Judges was Samuel. Hannah, Samuel's mother, had prayed to God for a long time to send her a son. God heard her prayer and she had a son whom she named Samuel, which means 'God has heard.'

Hannah took Samuel, at three years of age, to the temple and consecrated him to the Lord. One night, the Lord called Samuel three times, and Samuel finally understood that God was calling him to be His prophet. When Samuel grew up, he helped the people to listen to God and to follow Him.

David and Goliath

God told Samuel to go to Bethlehem and anoint a young boy, named David, to be king of Israel. Some time later, a war broke out between the Israelites, who were led by King Saul, and the Philistines. A terrible giant named Goliath dared any Israelite to fight him hand to hand. The Israelites were so frightened that none of them would come out to fight Goliath. But David said, "I will fight this Philistine!"

David picked five smooth stones, took his sling, and went forth to meet the giant. Goliath laughed at David, but David whirled a stone in his sling and flung it at the giant. The stone hit Goliath so hard that he fell to the ground. David cut off his head! After King Saul died, David was chosen king of Israel. King David ruled for 40 years, and Israel became a great kingdom.

The Temple of Solomon

After King David died, his son Solomon became king of Israel. One night the Lord appeared to Solomon and told him to ask for whatever he wanted. Solomon asked for the wisdom to rule his people with justice and goodness. The Lord was so pleased that He also gave Solomon riches, honor, and long life.

Solomon built a grand and beautiful temple for the Lord. When he dedicated the temple, Solomon offered to the Lord 22,000 oxen and 120,000 sheep. Thus he and all the Israelites dedicated the temple of the Lord.

Solomon wrote the Book of Proverbs as well as psalms and songs for the Lord. However, when Solomon grew old he fell into sin and oppressed his people. Solomon reigned over Israel for 40 years. He was buried in Jerusalem.

Jonah and the Whale

Jonah was a prophet who lived many years ago. One day God told Jonah, "Go to the great city of Nineveh and preach to the people, for it is very wicked." But Jonah did not want the people of Nineveh to repent, since they were enemies of Israel. So he sailed far away from there.

The Lord sent a great storm upon the sea, and Jonah told the sailors to throw him overboard, thinking that would stop the storm. They did so, and a great whale came and swallowed Jonah. Jonah begged God to free him, and after three days and nights, the whale spit Jonah out onto dry land.

Jonah then obeyed God and preached to the people of Nineveh. When the king of Nineveh and his people heard Jonah, they repented of their wickedness and turned back to God. Then God had mercy on them, and He spared their land.

Daniel and the Lions' Den

Daniel was only a boy when he and his other Hebrew friends were taken away from Israel into captivity in Babylon. God gave Daniel the ability to understand dreams, and he helped the king of Babylon understand his dream.

Later, a new king named Darius chose Daniel and two other men to help govern his kingdom. The two men were jealous of Daniel, so they convinced Darius to make a law that no one could worship any god but himself.

Daniel worshipped God, as he had always done, and the king had to throw him into a den of hungry lions. However, God sent an angel to shut the mouths of the lions. The king rejoiced when he saw that Daniel was unhurt, and he ordered his soldiers to remove Daniel from the lion's den. God delivered His servant Daniel because he trusted Him. Alleluia!

THE NEW TESTAMENT
The Annunciation

One day, God sent the angel Gabriel to the town of Nazareth, to a virgin named Mary, who was engaged to Joseph. Gabriel said to Mary, "Hail, full of grace! The Lord is with you!" Mary was troubled. The angel said, "Do not be afraid, Mary. You have found favor with God. Behold, you will conceive a son in your womb, and you shall call him Jesus. He will be great, the Son of the Most High God. He will rule over the house of Jacob forever." Mary said, "How can this be? I am a virgin!" The angel replied, "The Holy Spirit will come upon you, and the power of the Most High will overshadow you. Therefore the child to be born will be called holy, the Son of God."

Mary said, "I am the handmaid of the Lord. Let it be done unto me according to your word." With that the angel left her.

The Journey to Bethlehem

Some months later, the Roman ruler, Caesar Augustus, ordered that a census be taken to find out how many people lived in the world. Everyone had to go to their own town to be enrolled.

Joseph and Mary left Nazareth and journeyed to the city of David, called Bethlehem, because Joseph was of the house and family of David. Mary was very close to her time of delivery.

Joseph and Mary arrived in Bethlehem late one night, but when they got there every inn and house of that town was full, and they found no place to stay. Mary was very tired, and Joseph tried very hard to find a place. Finally Joseph found a little stable with a manger in it where the animals were fed. He did his best to make it comfortable for Mary, who laid down to rest.

The Birth of Jesus

That night, Mary gave birth to her son, Jesus. Mary wrapped her baby in warm clothing and laid him in the manger.

In the fields nearby, shepherds were watching their flocks when suddenly an angel of the Lord came to them in a bright light. The angel said to them, "Do not be afraid! Behold, I bring you good news of great joy: Today in the city of David a savior is born for you who is Messiah and Lord. This will be a sign for you: You will find a baby wrapped in swaddling clothes and lying in a manger."

Suddenly a great number of angels appeared, praising God and singing, "Glory to God in the highest, and on earth peace to all people of good will." The shepherds went in haste to Bethlehem, to see their new-born King.

The Gift of the Magi

At this time Wise Men, called Magi, traveled from far away to Jerusalem. They asked King Herod, "Where is the child the people call King of the Jews? We have seen his star in the sky, and have come to worship him."

The jealous King asked his learned men, "Where is the Messiah to be born?" They answered, "In Bethlehem, as it is written: 'You, Bethlehem, are not the least among the clans of Judah; since from you shall come a ruler who is to shepherd my people Israel.'"

The Magi set out, following the star until it stopped over the place where Jesus was. They found Jesus with his mother, Mary. They worshiped him, and gave him gifts of gold, frankincense, and myrrh. The Magi did not return to Herod, but left for home by another way.

The Finding of Jesus in the Temple

Every year Jesus went up with his parents to Jerusalem for the feast of Passover, as God had commanded the Jews to do when He delivered them from Egypt. When Jesus was twelve years old, Joseph and Mary went to the feast as usual. Afterwards, they returned home, but without their knowledge, Jesus remained behind.

When Joseph and Mary realized that Jesus was missing, they returned to Jerusalem. After three days they found him in the temple, listening to the teachers and asking them questions. Mary said, "Son, why have you done this to us? Your father and I have been so worried!" Jesus answered, "Did you not know I must be in my Father's house?" Then he returned to Nazareth with his parents, and he obeyed them in all things.

The Baptism of Jesus

John the Baptist was the cousin of Jesus. He
wore a garment of camel's skin, and lived in
the desert, praying to God with all his heart.
John baptized the people in the river Jordan
for the forgiveness of sins. When Jesus was 30
years old, he came to be baptized by John.
After Jesus was baptized, suddenly the sky
opened up, and he saw the Holy Spirit, in
the shape of a dove, come down from heaven
and rest upon him. The people around heard
a voice from heaven, which said, "This is my
Beloved Son, in whom I am well pleased."

John said, "Behold the Lamb of God, who
takes away the sin of the world. God told me,
'When you see the Holy Spirit descend like
a dove on someone, he is the one who will
baptize you with the Holy Spirit.' Now I have
seen and I testify that Jesus is the Son of God."

Jesus Calls His Apostles

The Holy Spirit led Jesus into the desert to be
tested. He returned, filled with the Holy Spirit
and power. John the Baptist saw him and said,
"Behold the Lamb of God, who takes away
the sin of the world!" Two of John's disciples,
Andrew and John, followed after Jesus. He
turned and said, "What are you looking for?"
They asked him, "Rabbi—Teacher—where are
you staying?" He replied, "Come and see."

Andrew told his brother Peter about Jesus, and
John told his brother James as well. Later, Jesus
found these men by the Sea of Galilee, for they
were fishermen. He said to them, "Come follow
me, and I will make you fishers of men."

At once the fishermen left their nets and
followed Jesus. Jesus called other men to
follow him as well, and soon he had twelve
apostles.

The Wedding at Cana

There was a wedding in the town of Cana, and Mary and Jesus and his disciples were there. The guests drank all the wine. Mary said to Jesus, "They have no wine." Jesus replied, "My hour has not yet come." Still, Mary knew he would do something, so she told the servers, "Do whatever he tells you."

In the banquet room there were six large stone jars, and Jesus told the servants, "Fill the jars with water." Then Jesus said, "Draw some out and take it to the headwaiter." The headwaiter tasted the water, which had become wine. He told the groom, "Usually people serve the good wine first, and then, when people have drunk a lot, they serve the lesser wine. But you have kept the good wine until now." Jesus did this first of his signs, and so revealed his glory, and his disciples began to believe in him.

The Sermon on the Mount

One day Jesus went up a mountain to teach his disciples and the people about God. He said to them, "Blessed are those who are poor, who trust in God, for the kingdom of heaven is theirs. Blessed are those who feel sad, for God will comfort them. Blessed are those who are quiet and humble, for the earth will be given to them. Blessed are those who want to be good, for they shall be satisfied. Blessed are those who help others with mercy, for mercy shall be theirs. Blessed are the pure of heart, for they will see God. Blessed are those who make peace, for they shall be called the children of God. Blessed are those who suffer for doing what is right, for the kingdom of heaven is theirs."

Jesus said, "Seek first the kingdom of God, and everything else will be given to you."

Jesus Cures a Leper

The people listened eagerly to Jesus, who told them the truth. When he came down the mountain, huge crowds followed him.

As Jesus walked along, a leper approached and knelt before him. Leprosy was a serious illness that caused a person's skin to become white and fall off. Lepers had to stay away from everyone, and call out a warning, "Unclean! Unclean!" "Please, Lord," the man said, "if you wish, you can make me clean." Jesus felt pity for the man. He stretched out his hand and touched him, and said, "I will do it. Be made clean." Immediately the leper was healed.

"Tell no one," Jesus said, "but show yourself to the priest, and offer the gift that Moses prescribed, and that will be proof for them."

Jesus Teaches His Disciples to Pray

Jesus loved to go away to quiet places and pray. One day, when he had finished praying, one of his followers said, "Lord, teach us to pray."

Jesus answered, "When you pray, say: Our Father, who art in heaven, hallowed be Thy name. Thy kingdom come, Thy will be done, on earth as it is in heaven. Give us this day our daily bread, and forgive us our sins as we forgive those who sin against us, and do not put us to the test, but deliver us from the evil one."

Jesus said, "If you forgive others, your heavenly Father will forgive you. But if you do not forgive others, neither will your Father forgive you for what you do."

Jesus Calms the Storm

After teaching and healing many people, Jesus got into a boat with his disciples to cross the Sea of Galilee. Jesus was very tired, so he curled up in the boat and fell fast asleep.

Suddenly a violent storm came up on the sea. The waves grew higher and higher. The disciples did their best to keep the boat afloat, but when they realized it was sinking they felt terrified. They went to Jesus and woke him, saying, "Lord, save us! We are perishing!"

Jesus said to them, "Why are you terrified? Do you not have faith?" Then he got up and rebuked the winds and the sea.

Suddenly the rains stopped falling, the winds stopped blowing, and the sea grew calm. The disciples asked each other, "What sort of man is this? Even the winds and the sea obey him!"

The Miracle of the Loaves and the Fishes

Many people traveled a long way to see and hear Jesus. One time more than 5,000 people had been with him all day, and they were hungry. The apostles were concerned, and they told Jesus, "Send the people to buy food." Jesus answered, "Give them food yourselves." The disciples replied, "There is a boy here who has five barley loaves and two fish; but what good are these for so many?"

Jesus said, "Have the people sit down." Then he took the loaves and the fish, looked up to heaven, blessed the food, and gave the loaves and fish to his disciples to give to the people. Everyone ate till they were full, and the disciples collected twelve baskets of leftovers! Just as Jesus had promised, God provides what we need, and more, when we put our trust in Him.

Jesus Names Peter as the Rock

One day Jesus asked his followers, "Who do people say that that I am?" They replied, "Some say you are John the Baptist, or Elijah, or one of the prophets."

He replied, "But who do you say I am?" Simon Peter replied, "You are the Messiah, the Son of the living God."

Jesus said, "Blessed are you, Simon, son of Jonah. For flesh and blood has not revealed this to you, but my heavenly Father revealed this to you. And so I say to you, you are Peter, and upon this rock I will build my church, and the gates of hell shall not hold out against it. I will give you the keys to the kingdom of heaven. Whatever you bind on earth shall be bound in heaven; and whatever you loose on earth shall be loosed in heaven."

Jesus Heals a Little Girl

Jesus was teaching the people, when suddenly a man named Jairus rushed to him, fell down on his knees before Jesus and cried, "My little girl is dying. Please, Jesus, come and heal her!" Jesus followed Jairus, and as they approached his home, some people said to Jairus, "Your daughter is dead." Jesus turned to Jairus and said to him, "Be not afraid. Just have faith."

When they came into the house, many people were crying and wailing loudly. Jesus said, "Do not weep. The child is not dead, but asleep." Then he took his closest apostles and Jairus and his wife into the room. Jesus walked to the bed and took the girl by the hand.

He said, "Little girl, I say to you, arise!" Immediately she got up and began to walk around. When the people saw what Jesus had done, they were completely amazed.

Jesus Blesses the Children

Little children loved to be around Jesus because they knew he loved them. His warm smile and big hugs made them feel good. And Jesus loved the little children. He liked telling them stories about farmers and fishermen, shepherds and kings. He would listen to them, and they would listen to him.

One day some mothers and fathers brought their children to Jesus so he might lay his hands on them and bless them. The apostles cried, "Stop! Jesus is too busy to see your children!" But Jesus said, "Let the children come to me, and do not stop them. My kingdom belongs to such as these, and unless you become like little children, you will not enter it." Then the children all ran up to Jesus. He laughed with them, blessed them, and gave them back to their parents.

The Good Samaritan

One day a student of the Law asked Jesus, "What must I do to receive eternal life?" Jesus replied, "Love God with all your heart, and love your neighbor as you love yourself." "But who is my neighbor?" asked the scholar.

Jesus replied, "A man was attacked by robbers. They stripped and beat him and left him half-dead. A priest and a Levite saw him and passed on the opposite side. Then, a Samaritan traveler saw the wounded man and was filled with compassion. He poured oil and wine over his wounds and bandaged them. He put him on his own donkey and took him to an inn. He gave money to the innkeeper, saying, 'Take care of him. I shall repay you when I return.' Which of these three, do you think, was neighbor to the man?" The scholar answered, "The one who treated him with mercy." Jesus replied, "Then go and do the same."

The Forgiving Father

Jesus told another story: "A rich man had two sons. The younger son said, 'Father, give me my share of your estate. I want to leave home.' The father was sad, but he gave his son the money. The younger son went far away and spent all his money. Now broke, he took work caring for pigs. He thought, 'My father's servants have all they want to eat, but I am starving! I shall return to my father and say, "I have sinned and do not deserve to be called your son. Treat me as one of your servants."'

"While the son was still a long way off, his father saw him. He ran to his son, hugged him and kissed him. He said to his servants, 'Give him the finest robe, and put a ring on his finger and sandals on his feet! Let's have a big party, because my son was dead, and has come to life! He was lost, and is found.'"

Blind Bartimaeus

One day, Jesus and his disciples came to a town named Jericho. A blind man named Bartimaeus sat by the road, begging. He asked someone what was happening. "Jesus is passing by!" they told him. Bartimaeus cried out, "Jesus, Son of David, have pity on me!" "Be quiet!" the people told him. "You're making too much noise!" But Bartimaeus cried out louder, "Have pity on me!"

Jesus stopped. "Call the man," he said. Friends of Bartimaeus led him to Jesus. Jesus asked, "What do you want me to do for you?" Bartimaeus said, "Master, I want to see." Jesus smiled and said, "Go your way, my friend. Your faith has saved you." Immediately Bartimaeus' eyes were opened, and he was able to see. He rejoiced and shouted, "I can see! I can see!" Then he followed Jesus on the way.

The Good Shepherd

Jesus said, "Once upon a time there was a shepherd who had many sheep. He knew each of them by name. Every day he took them out into the fields and meadows so they could eat good rich grass and drink cool water.

"One day, a little lamb ran away from the other sheep and got lost. When the shepherd realized his lamb was missing, he left his other sheep and went to find it. He looked up in the mountains and down by the streams. Finally he found the frightened little lamb, put it on his shoulders, and brought it home.

"The shepherd said, 'Rejoice with me, for I have found my sheep that was lost!'" Jesus said, "I am the Good Shepherd. I know my sheep, and they know me, and they follow me. If they get lost, I search for them and find them and bring them back home to me."

Jesus said to his apostles, "It is time for us to go up to Jerusalem. The Feast of the Passover is near." Two of Jesus' disciples brought him a donkey, covered it with their cloaks, and helped him to mount. As Jesus rode into Jerusalem, a great crowd of excited people came out to meet him. Some of them laid their cloaks on the ground where Jesus was passing. Other people cut down palm branches to lay on the ground before him, and little children scattered flowers at his feet.

The disciples of Jesus and the people began to praise God joyfully for all the great and wonderful deeds that Jesus had done. Many of them waved palm and olive branches and cried out, "Hosanna! Blessed is He who comes in the name of the Lord! Hosanna!" They all entered Jerusalem with great joy.

Jesus Cleanses the Temple

Jesus entered the temple in Jerusalem, where many merchants were exchanging money, and buying and selling. Jesus became angry, and he said to them, "It is written in the prophet Isaiah, 'My house shall be called a house of prayer,' but you have made it a den of thieves!" He drove out the moneychangers from the temple, in order that it might be a place of prayer and peace.

While he was there, Jesus looked at the rich people putting their contributions into the offering box. Then he saw a poor widow, who had no husband to support her. She put two small coins into the box. Jesus asked his disciples, "Do you see this poor widow? She has given more to God than all the others. They gave from their wealth, what they had left over, but she has given from her poverty, all she had to live on."

The Last Supper

On the night of the Passover, Jesus sat down
with his apostles for the Passover meal. The
devil had already put it into the heart of Judas
Iscariot to betray Jesus. Judas left in the dark.

During the meal, Jesus took the bread, blessed
it, broke it, and gave it to his disciples saying,
"Take and eat; this is my body." Then he took
a chalice of wine, gave thanks, and passed it
around, saying, "Drink this, all of you, for
this is my blood, to be poured out for the
forgiveness of sins. Do this in memory of me."
Jesus and his apostles sang a hymn of praise
to God, and went out to the Mount of Olives.
Jesus said to them, "Tonight your faith in me
will be tested, and you will all be scattered. But
after I have been raised up, I will go before you
into Galilee."

The Agony in the Garden

Jesus went out with his disciples to the Garden of Gethsemane. He took Peter, James, and John with him further, and he became very sad and troubled. Jesus asked them to stay awake and pray. Then he moved away a little bit and knelt down, praying, "Father, if You are willing, You can take this suffering away from me; but may Your Will be done."

Jesus went back to his disciples three times, but each time he found them asleep. He said, "Could you not watch one hour with me?"

Meanwhile, the temple priests had paid Judas Iscariot to betray Jesus. Judas came into the garden with a crowd of soldiers and he kissed Jesus. Jesus said, "Judas, would you betray me with a kiss?" He said to the crowd, "Have you come after me as against a robber? I was with you many days, and you did not arrest me; but this is the time for the power of darkness." Then the soldiers took Jesus, and his friends ran away.

Jesus is Condemned to Death

When morning came, the guards brought Jesus before the elders, chief priests, and scribes. Many witnesses told false stories about him. Jesus did not answer a word. Finally the high priest asked him, "Are you the Messiah, the Son of God?" Jesus answered, "I am." They all cried, "He is worthy of death!" They led him away to Pontius Pilate, the Roman governor. Pilate had his soldiers scourge Jesus and put a crown of thorns on his head. Then Pilate condemned Jesus to death.

The soldiers laid a heavy cross on Jesus' shoulders and made him carry it up to the Mount of Calvary, where he was to be crucified. Many people shouted at Jesus and made fun of him, but others felt very sad for Jesus and were sorrowful as he staggered by.

Jesus Dies on the Cross

When they arrived at Calvary, the soldiers nailed Jesus to the cross. On top of the cross Pilate had written the letters INRI, which meant "Jesus of Nazareth, King of the Jews." Jesus looked up to heaven from the cross, and prayed, "Father, forgive them, for they do not know what they are doing."

As Jesus hung on the cross, he saw his mother, Mary, standing at the foot of the cross with his beloved apostle, John. Jesus said to his mother, "Woman, behold your son." Then to John he said, "Behold your mother." And from that hour John took Mary into his home.

Jesus then said, "I thirst!" A soldier dipped a sponge in some common wine, and raised it to Jesus. Jesus said, "It is finished. Father, into Your hands I commit my spirit!" And bowing his head, Jesus died.

Jesus Rises from the Dead!

Jesus was buried in a tomb which had been sealed with a huge stone across the entrance. Very early in the morning on the first day of the week, as soldiers were guarding the tomb, the earth began to shake violently. In the middle of the earthquake, an angel of the Lord descended from heaven, approached the tomb, rolled away the stone, and sat upon it. He looked like lightening and his clothing was white as snow. The guards fell down in fear.

Suddenly, in a burst of great light, Jesus arose from the dead! He shined brighter than the sun. The soldiers cried out and ran away. Mary Magdalene and some other women who had come to anoint the body of Jesus saw an angel. "Do not be afraid!" the angel said. "I know you are seeking Jesus. He is not here, for he is risen, just as he said. Go tell his disciples!"

Jesus Ascends into Heaven

After his resurrection, Jesus stayed on the earth for forty days, speaking to his disciples about the kingdom of God. Jesus was now ready to leave the earth and return to his Father in heaven.

Jesus told his apostles, "Do not depart from Jerusalem, but wait there for 'the promise of the Father' about which I have spoken to you. John baptized with water, but in a few days you will be baptized with the Holy Spirit.

"You will receive power when the Holy Spirit comes upon you. Then you will be my witnesses in Jerusalem, throughout Judea and Samaria, and to the ends of the earth."

When Jesus had said this, he blessed his disciples, and ascended up into heaven. As they were looking on, a cloud took him away out of their sight.

The Holy Spirit Descends Upon the Apostles

After Jesus ascended into heaven, the apostles returned to Jerusalem. Mother Mary was with them, as were other disciples—about 120 in all. When the day of Pentecost came, they were all in one room together. Suddenly a noise like a strong driving wind came from the sky and filled the room. Tongues as of fire appeared, which parted and rested on each one of them. All of them were filled with the Holy Spirit! They began to speak in different tongues, as the Spirit enabled them to proclaim.

When the Jewish people heard the apostles and disciples praising God in different languages, they were greatly amazed. Peter stood up with the apostles and proclaimed to all the good news that God had raised Jesus from the dead. He had made him both Lord and Messiah. That very day 3,000 people were baptized. The Church was born!

The Gospel Spreads to the Whole World

The apostles preached the Gospel everywhere, and invited all people to receive Jesus as their Savior. God changed the hearts of those who believed, especially a man named Saul who became the great Saint Paul. The apostles consecrated other men to continue their work. From that time down to this very day, God has continued to offer to all people the gift of His salvation and love. This He does through Jesus and through the Church, His family on earth.